I0494851

MANAGE THAT I.T. PROJECT

ISBN: 978-1-4717-5304-6

Copyright   © Andreas Sofroniou   2012

Copyright   © Andreas Sofroniou   2012

MANAGE THAT I.T. PROJECT

ISBN: 978-1-4717-5304-6

CONTENTS: PAGE:

FOREWORD

There can be little doubt that information systems and computing in general will become increasingly important in the years ahead. This book is, therefore, aiming to fill a gap in the current business and tutorial literature.

The '*MANAGE THAT INFORMATION TECHNOLOGY PROJECT*' book has been designed for the business person, for the student and the computer professional who needs a detailed overview of projects and the systems involved.

The book explores the fundamental aspects of operational computing and the development of new information systems. Current systems are discussed according to their structure and the book focuses on further developments in information technology, and their planning.

In writing the book, the author is mostly concerned with the development and the managing of systems and people in multi-national corporations, software houses, government departments, the European Union Commissions, and academia.

EurIng Dr Andreas Sofroniou has close links with business systems and their development and the system engineering profession as a whole. He has developed numerous systems and managed a variety of applications and systems people, including Year 2000 projects.

It is the author's wish that the reader thoroughly enjoys reading the contents of this book.

1. I.T. AND PEOPLE INVOLVED

This book is mostly concerned with the management of projects in Information Technology and the people involved in such development; the individuals who work on their own and those who work in groups to design systems applicable to users, the system practitioners who may be employed by multi-national corporations, software houses, government departments, European Union Commissions, or academia.

Information Technology as a service is given to all types of businesses, in any environment. As a tool at work, an Information Technology department deals with individual problems, ranging from difficulties within job responsibilities, rifts and business inadequacies, including systems, operational problems and the people involved in such activities.

The book will assist operational groups of people, in various sections of Information Technology. Based on the contents, projects can be planned and prepared to suit the users, their interactions, systems development, and systems methodologies.

The modern Information Technology Project Manager attempts to merge the latest developments in human sciences and advanced technology. The combination of both, gives a service applicable to the systems user and his/her working surroundings.

In Information Technology, the major theme is the responsibility to the system user, the individual, and the company; to help with their problems and requirements in system development. The emergent technologies and the pace of change are placing increasing importance upon organisations and individuals being finely tuned, in performance terms. This does not just happen, but has to be worked at.

MANAGE THAT I.T. PROJECT

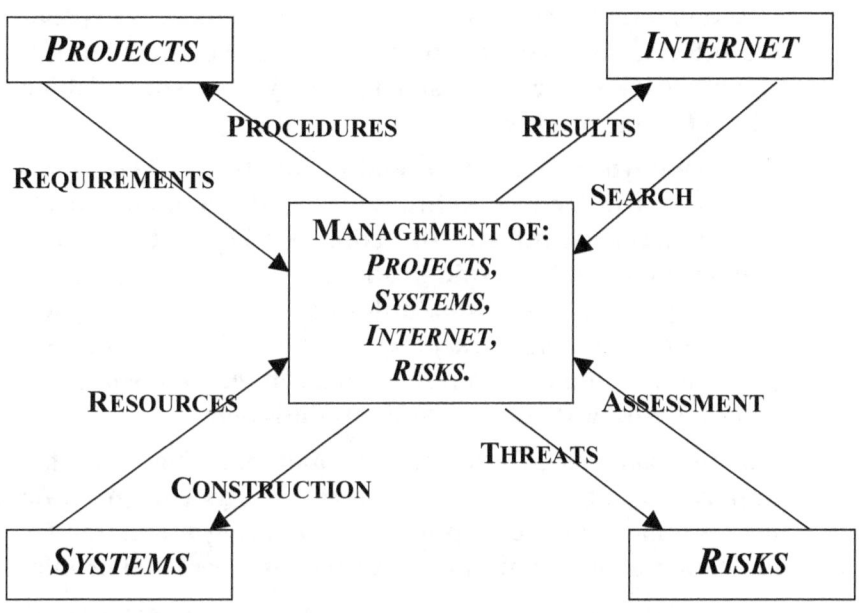

The Information Technology Project Manager's role is to provide a service in computing which will assist in developing skills, diagnose, and treat discontinuities which affect the performance of the systems. In Information Technology, the commercial, industrial, and human expertise embraces the whole range of services. Technology in business environments, directing and management techniques, systems designing, personnel selection, counselling, training, and individual development, production methods and artificial intelligence.

Many organisational and personnel problems may be solved. The project manager of systems offers advice and undertakes assignments relating to all aspects of information technology, including strategic, business and data analysis, systems and database designing, networking, hardware and software selection and systems users' training. Within an organisation, the Information Technology expertise can be offered as an ad-hoc advisory service, as a short term systems specialist, or on a long term project basis.

This book will prove very useful to the Project Manager who wishes to use modern skills, such as the human aspects of system management and directing, setting of tasks, project management, and the state-of-the-art in computing, as a tool. The responsibilities within information technology and the systems engineering areas, include the understanding of user personality, human-computer interaction, and comparative methods within structured systems designing.

On the academic, educational, and training aspect, the importance of a person as a whole system programme professional must be emphasised, this being the major factor in dealing with organisational, system and personal problems.

In the last few years, modern universities prepare their courses to suit the business environment and towards the professional accreditation of the appropriate computing institution. The whole venture of academia and the engineering institutions is seen by businesses as a pro for a continuous human development policy. This ensures high quality employment opportunities, secured in growth industries at the forefront of technological changes.

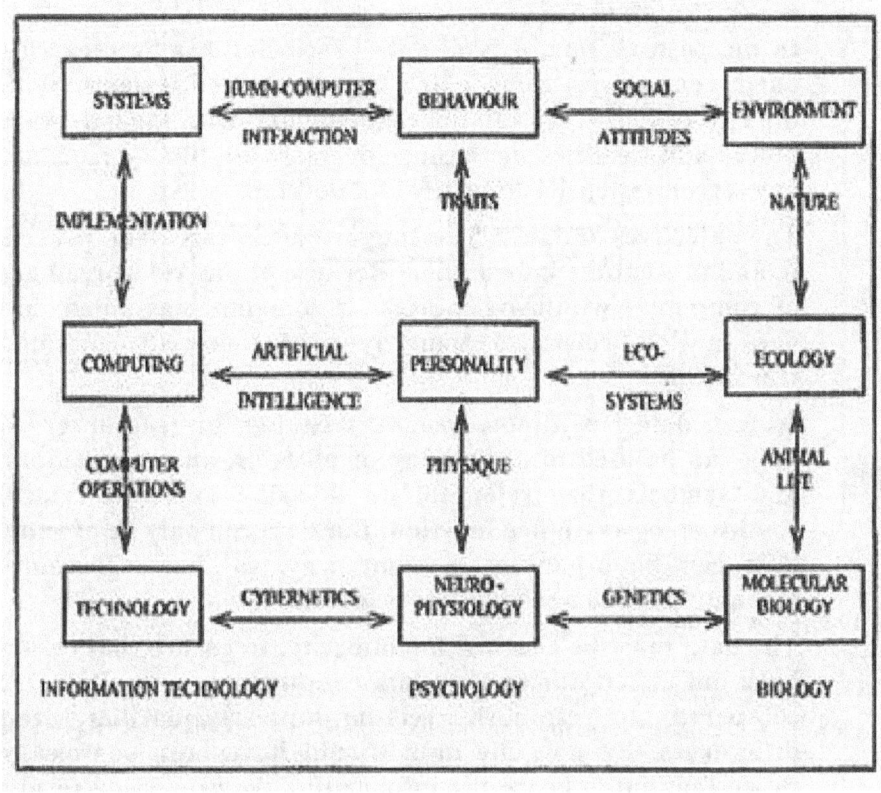

2. PROJECT MANAGEMENT

In the past, the majority of data processing has been carried out by companies using batch style computer systems. With the cost of hardware rapidly reducing and with the hardware power and facilities increasing inversely, on-line systems are now becoming easier to justify and develop.

The objectives of data processing are to capture data, process it, and present the information. Because of the widespread use of computers within business, it is sometimes assumed that data always refers to some type of financially oriented transaction.

In fact, data has a more general meaning. In general terms, data can be used to denote any or all facts, numbers, letters, and symbols that refer to, or describe an object, idea, condition, or any other function. But data can only be of value if it can be organised in some way, so that it becomes meaningful to somebody - this is information.

The data must be checked for integrity, to ensure that errors have not arisen during any data capture processes. Data are compared to establish relationships, similarities, and differences. By now the data should have been completely processed, but to be proper information the processing results must be presented in such a way that it has relevance and meaning. Finally, the information must be produced on a medium that is legible.

In years bygone, on-line systems of any form have been difficult to justify because of the cost of:

- additional hardware needed to sustain speedy response times,

- systems software needed to support individual terminal activity,

- additional design overhead for systems assurance.

With hardware power increasing and their costs reducing rapidly, these objectives are now disappearing.

Indeed, the justification for modern applications must be much easier now, when their benefits include:

- speedier data entry,
- reduced data error rates,
- faster processing cycles,
- quick response to user enquiries.

Of all the major problems encountered in computing, the most difficult is the management of the systems and their development. Unlike any engineering or architectural drawings, the systems cannot be visibly represented as a model. Any building or machine can be shown as a set of drawings and as a three dimensional model, but the design and the build of the system cannot be seen, nor can it be represented on top of a desk.

In the case of an architectural concept, the designer will draw the plans and will supervise and delegate the tasks to builders to construct in a fashion, as close to perfect logistics as possible.

In modern Information Technology and computing in general, structured methodologies are used, where dataflow diagrams can be drawn, data can be modelled and at the end of the logical phase, the system can be prototyped and programmed.

This brings forward the problem of project managing, delegating, and guiding those who analyse the business requirements and the data on which the information is based, the professionals who proceed with the design based on the requirements and those who program and implement the required system.

In most cases, these activities are under one roof. Mainly, three different professions passing details to each other at the end of each developmental stage:

- Analysis,
- Designing.
- Programming.

The Information Technology Project Manager will need to know what each step of development involves and at every phase what the professional system practitioner is doing. As in every other project, tasks need to be based on timescales and the financial implication to remain close to the budgets.

In commercial computing the financial costs for developing a new system are in six figures and in many cases where additional hardware and software are to be acquired, one project can be in the region of millions of pounds. To cope with such enormities of resources and the correct availability of business information, an organisation relies completely on the professional knowledge of its system project manager and those who participate in the construction of the projects.

The media frequently report failures of systems and frustrations in computers at large. More often within companies, disappointments in systems are such that the computer department is totally isolated from other business activities. Yet, there are those companies whose total running of their business is based on the smooth running of their computer systems; profitability and revenue always ahead of their competitors.

But, it is also true to say that with all modern computing and devices, industry still suffers, or outputs could be improved, if only the computer department could design and operate a system the way the users work and based on the company's requirements.

The system's project person is aware of these problems and yet cannot stretch his/her know-how any more than is already done. Imagine the various professionals under one roof, the complexity of designing and constructing systems, of the housekeeping involved, of the running and maintenance of all these sections.

If an organisation has many departments to enable it to function, so does the computer environment. In a superimposed mode, the Information Technology Manager has just as many sections to look after, admittedly on a smaller scale, but just as complex. Humans, machines, finances, stresses, productions, outputs, man-machine relationships, all in one department, just as much as any overall organisation is facing.

The I.T. Manager relies on management skills, systems knowledge, and various other business methods in order to give a good service to everybody in the company. The subject covers business computing and its management, the development of new systems, the implementation, and their running.

The Project Manager in computing is aware of actual examples and will draw on projects and experience gained in building large and moderate systems based on what the users require, their problems, the solutions and their training in ensuring the success of the new system, or additional information technology modules.

In the first place, the expertise of those involved must cover the last generation of computing (which systems are still operating in many international organisations), its successes and its failures and the running in company environments. This includes the mainframe-based systems, the advent of PCs (Personal Computers) and their impact on networking and distributed processing, expert systems, and artificial intelligence.

These, inevitably will be supported by training and experience in Structured Methodologies, a comparative study into methods, the use of the predominant systems architectures and a method for 'Rapid Building' system engineering.

Modern systems engineering, concentrates on the training aspect, the psychology of users, motivation and delegating specific to the computer departments, the interviewing techniques in gathering the information on current systems, the cataloguing of the problems and requirements, the appropriate solutions and their incorporation into the design of the required system.

Regarding the newcomers to the commercial computing professions, organisations rely on aspiring young graduates. With all good will they bring with them and with all their ambitions for the yuppie incomes, graduates still need the specialised training in computing and systems applications to business requirements.

It must be said that academia has progressed enormously in computing during the last ten years, but business needs differ from that of university research and studies. Graduates who enter the companies' surroundings find that they are unprepared for the demand of creating and using commercial systems in large organisations.

3. MANAGING SYSTEMS

The reader must remember that the construction of a system is as complex as a house built in a swamp. It requires careful planning and design. Just as a house must have an architect's plan, so does a system. It must have requirements, system objectives, and a blueprint.

In general, it must be well noticed that every system structured is an answer to the users' problems and requirements. The solutions will be based on the studies of the current systems, manual and computerised and the problems and requirements catalogue.

The design of the system will be based on how the users work and what suits the overall business environment. Whilst analysing the users' needs, the system analyst will proceed with the logical stages, by listening, interviewing, and having Walkthroughs and reviews with users and colleagues.

Prior to proceeding into the physical stages, the system project manager involved will seek approval from the appropriate groups of people. Within the physical stages and during the construction of the system, the system builders will test and make the necessary alterations to the modules being implemented.

The users' systems acceptance will include all the necessary documentation and all the training and support required to ensure that the new system or module is successful.

The illustration of the overall computing environment, (on the following page) can help in unravelling these complexities. The hierarchical diagram represents computing in large organisations. Within IT five major modules are included in a structured mode. Every module is diagrammatically represented, at different levels.

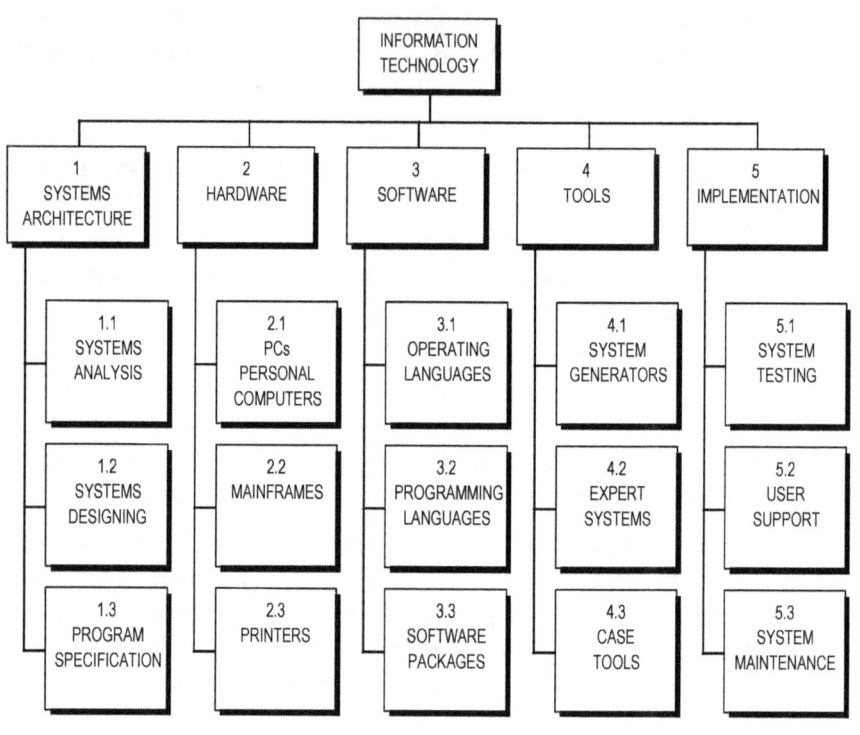

4. SYSTEMS ARCHITECTURE

The background of structured analysis and designing as an information technology methodology, a technique-driven approach, started in 1972. Between 1980 and 1982, Gane and Sarson and Yourdon methodologies were extensively used. In 1983, business started using the information engineering automated version. By 1989, the development paths underwent further evolution. In 1992, the business re-engineering and object-oriented versions were introduced.

The need to control and manage the ever-increasing amounts of all organisational data being created, particularly computer-generated data, has gained recognition. However, because data management automates the processes used within a company, implementation is not easy. Several data management suppliers have begun requesting that a full systems and business analysis is undertaken prior to system implementation.

Evidently, existing processes show not only where they need to be changed but also determine exactly what the data management system is required to do within each unique organisation. It, therefore, provides the platform for successful systems architecture and management introduction and avoids the many pitfalls that so many companies have experienced in attempting to develop and install a new management system.

Rapid prototyping is gaining acceptance. Companies are using this method to obtain system design models in weeks rather than months, dramatically reducing lead-times and enabling better decisions and choice of system modules to be made.

A Systems Project Manager in his/her approach defines the whole project, modularises it into manageable sections and proceeds in a logical manner according to the clear principles of user involvement.

The tasks are always broken down into structured goal-oriented and meaningful units of work. The end result of the structured sets of tasks is applicable to the development path of:

- **Information Strategy Planning,**
- **Business Area Analysis,**
- **Business Design/Technical Design,**
- **Construction,**
- **Transition,**
- **Production.**

The above stages can be used by Analysts, Designers, Project Managers, Directors and Trainers in information technology methods to suit the technical and the user environment.

New techniques have been introduced that dramatically reduce the time taken to solve business and system problems. The result is that it is now possible to take the requirements, analyse, and view the results in days or weeks, rather than months. This, of course, makes analysis possible and cost-effective within the design process, rather than a special system task.

Recent years have seen further development in business and systems analysis software. Product releases of leading software houses have not only made systems architecture easier for everyday system engineers, but faster too. Closer links to CASE (Computer-aided Software Engineering) systems have made analysis simpler, while new interfaces make analysis understandable to users.

The term systems analysis is used in many computer installations in different ways. In fact, for most development projects it means the following:

- fact finding,
- operational analysis,
- business system design.

System analysis for an organisation means that the analyst has more detailed work to do by establishing with the users that there is a justification for developing a new system.

5. DESIGNING SYSTEMS

The interface between the user and a computer system has always been an important design factor. In interactive computer systems the interface (the dialogue) can influence not only the system's efficiency, but also its acceptability to the user.

The significance of effective dialogue design has its advantages and disadvantages:

- computer initiated dialogues are initially effective for the novice user, but quickly fall into disfavour when the user becomes more familiar with the system,

- equally, 'short-hand' user initiated dialogues can only be used effectively by an experienced user.

Therefore, the first aspect of interface design is to determine who will be using the system and how frequently they will be using it.

It may be necessary to have two sets of dialogues for the same system. One for the trainees and a 'short-hand' version for experienced staff.

The user psychology here is extremely important. The interface between the user and the system must be an extension of the way the user does his/her work. Any dialogue which causes deviation from this, will cause frustration and ultimately dislike for the system.

The second aspect of dialogue design is to ensure that the system is friendly and responsive.

Friendly means that the:

- screen formats are easy to read, data entry areas are clearly identified and error conditions are highlighted,

- computer displays messages on the screens giving the status of user initiated functions.

Responsive means that the computer should react to a user's request within a given response time, which is normally a low number of seconds.

In summary, the design of the system is significant because:

- it affects the character of the overall systems design,
- it directly affects user acceptability,
- once committed to a design it is expensive to change.

The new technology is introducing techniques which are changing the way organisations work, as opposed to just addressing existing tasks. To successfully implement and apply the systems tools requires extensive education and it is this that is currently presenting the biggest hurdles for companies.

Computer security has become a challenge dominated by the improvements to the technology of computers. Techniques are being developed to make access to systems harder. In recent years, much work has been done to make the computer recognise individual characteristics, unique to the user, such as a signature, a fingerprint, or even the genetic print of DNA.

With users and companies becoming more dependent upon computer systems, the privacy and reliability of such systems are becoming critical aspects of design. Systems Assurance, a term which is currently popular, of a system embraces the parts of systems design which reduce the risk of both the fraudulent use of the system and lengthy recovery times in the event of a system's failure.

In many companies, one of the few problems that has to be resolved quickly, is:

- privacy, the fraudulent entry of data,
- policing, a system must be more than reporting violation, it must include effective restricted access at varying levels, to different users,

- recording access violations.

Users and companies are becoming more and more dependent upon resilience of computer-based systems. Failures due to:

- telecommunications,
- hardware,
- software.

Whichever the cause of the failure, the user will expect that the system can be recovered quickly and that the applications are free from data corruption.

Inconsistencies within applications can result in:

- the user losing confidence in the system,
- lengthy investigation into the cause of failure,
- protected systems down time whilst the data sets are reconstructed from source documentation.

Therefore, one significant aspect of recovery is the time taken to reconstruct application data sets. The most straightforward method of recovering is to duplicate them by backup. The advantage of a backup is that recovery after failure is extremely fast.

In various sensitive applications, frequent auditing is recommended. As a minimum, a daily control report should be produced, reconciling balances on the opening and closing versions of data sets. This report should, also, show in detail the origins of all transactions processed during the reporting period.

With the number of computer applications continuing to grow and with a similar increase in the number of people using them, a new type of back-up service is needed. To meet the demand, a number of companies have introduced guides to their applications, which include catalogues on CD ROM. The catalogue, in fact, serves as a comprehensive system engineering tool.

Details on system applications, specifications, and service requirements are made available to all users. If a user is not sure what documents are needed, he/she can start by looking at the full index.

Companies are even making available dedicated internal e-mail messages and Internet pages. The latter being interactive and intelligent. Newsletters are published, which keep the users informed of new product developments, interesting applications, and other IT activities.

The widespread use of computers throughout business and the rapid growth of Internet connectivity mean that computer security should concern all organisations.

However, it involves more topics than might be supposed; ranging from the technicalities of protecting networks, and mobile systems, through the legalities of computer crime and corporate responsibility, to the politics of registering and protecting encryption keys.

Extremely sophisticated identification systems now exist that can read retina patterns, fingerprints and infra-red emissions from faces.

One simple measure to prevent unauthorised outsiders dialling into the system is to install dial-back modems. However, this security measure is easy to side-step. Likewise, calling-line identification, which permits the computer to identify the calling number and refuse access if it not recognised, can be bypassed by the experienced people.

Encryption is essential for the transmission of any material passing down the line. A simple method is to employ software which uses the same code at either end to encode and decode data. The next level is to impose a code of the day, using an encryption device card which is synchronised with a similar calculator card within the network.

The most complex form of encryption available is the digital signature. Each user, has a private key linked to a public key made available on an electronic notice board. The user encodes the message with the private key and the message can be decoded by anyone holding the allocated public key. However, any message encoded with the public key can be decoded only by the holder of the private key.

Developing large systems require a range of software to achieve the overall systems objective. Depending upon the application and hardware types, this range of software at best could be totally packaged, or at worst may need to be completely written specially for the system.

Software in a project is like a jigsaw puzzle. Each piece fulfils a role and each piece must integrate with other pieces to make the complete system.

The basic types of software used are:

- applications software,
- conversational software,
- database management software,
- system development software,
- network software,
- system support software.

Applying hardware and software knowledge to system engineering and the development of systems enables System Architects to choose individual applications from a range of developers and bring these together into a single system that best meets the needs of the company and its tasks, transparently, sharing data. It also enables standard software, such as spreadsheets, word-processing, presentation packages, and databases, to be linked to engineering software.

The flexibility this gives is far better for users than the traditional closed systems environment that forms the basis of many engineering software packages.

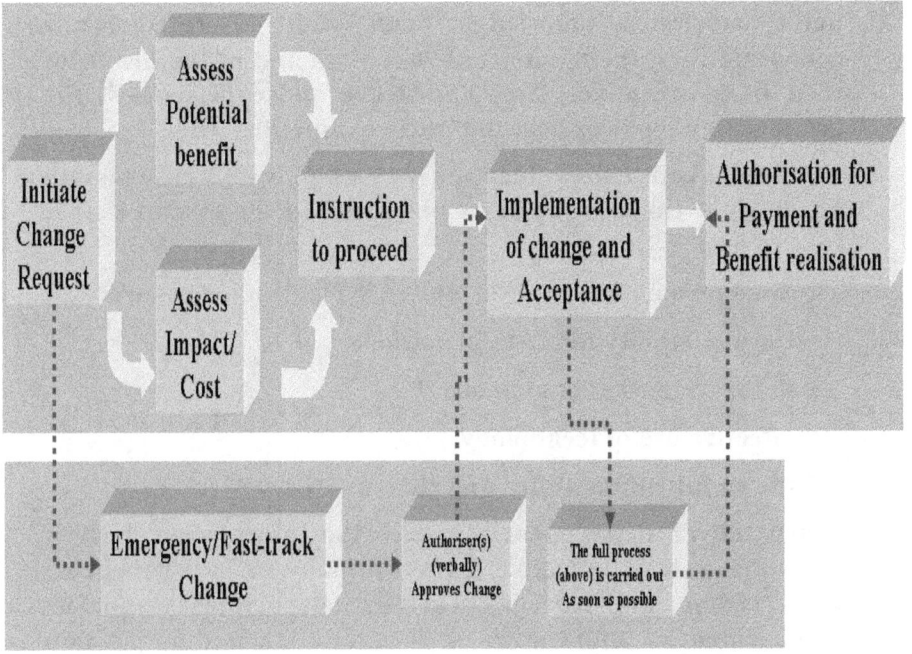

6. MANAGING SYSTEMS DEVELOPMENT

The majority of organisations recognise that the effective use of information is vital to their success. Successful companies build enormous knowledge bases that reside in their corporate files, their information centres and in the brains of their busy executives. This knowledge and experience is the organisation's power base and their competitive edge.

To remain competitive they must be able to find information at the right time, in the right place and in the format that is easy to use.

The management of the information systems must ensure:

- the availability of the information,
- the services that enable this,
- effective use of technology,
- the supply of the skills and time needed.

When the IT department manages the information derived from the systems, effectively, the company in turn gains real value from information. The IT department and its management of information must maintain a leading position in the specialised world of commercial computing.

The IT department will certainly benefit by having a network of specialists providing knowledge, experience, and technical skills to suit most types of company demands.

In managing IT professionally, the benefits will include the:

- capturing of the knowledge already in the organisation,
- making this knowledge accessible to those running the company,
- developing the appropriate strategic plans and systems,
- protection of the information supplied by the systems,
- accuracy and recoverability of all data,

- recruitment, training and developing the system engineers.

Instant access to corporate information means better decisions, reduced costs, and increased profits. To facilitate such a service, the IT department must work with a wide range of other departments and their staff. Many of the users are looking for help or advice from the information management area.

This means that the IT staff must be prepared to undertake all sizes of projects, their development, and the management of such systems. This entails a project management system which, together with the chosen methodology, will ensure the success of the information services.

Many users believe that a project must involve computers in some way. However, a much broader view is required when one considers that a project is set up to deliver a business product. In other words, a projects temporary, which only exists to deliver something considered worthwhile to the business.

The resulting product may be for any application (manual or otherwise, clerical, management style, production of goods, engineering in general), including a computer system. In this case, the environment created and the work done to deliver the product is a project.

In some cases, projects may not deliver what was expected and costly investment produces few benefits. It is little wonder that things go wrong and projects fail, not because people are ineffective, but because of the sheer complexity of project management.

Some of the problems which may be familiar to management at all levels are:

- no standard approach to project management,
- lack of communication,

- inadequate planning,
- unclear project objectives,
- uncontrolled change,
- shortage of experienced project managers,
- inadequate team building,
- inefficient staff motivation,
- poor quality standards.

Over the years it has become recognised that there is a common thread running through the management of projects. Much of this is common sense and it is the formulation of this rational thinking and management good practice, into a structure, which gives rise to project methods.

There are many project management methods available, each of which is characterised by the way in which it provides principles, procedures, and techniques for the management of projects. Methods utilise existing standard techniques as well as introducing their own unique features.

The number of project failures can be dramatically reduced by the proper application of a structured project management method. A method which provides project management principles, and processes to address the problems.

Structured management methods have evolved in private and government sectors since the late seventies. Such management methods are offered as publicly available open products. This means that it is available to anyone and can be used without permission to apply it and without license, or fee of any kind.

A number of project management methods provide a variety of approaches. Traditional project management and other management methods plan and control against a list of activities. Some specially designed for the information systems project environment. Such procedures are applied to many types and sizes of project. This, therefore, gives the advantage of common standards being applied to the management of systems projects.

Using a management method will ensure that a system is built for the users and for the benefit of the business. Quality is of paramount importance to all IT departments. There are a few official national and international standards in information management, so an important feature of the structured management method approach is to create a de facto environment where standards can interrelate as they evolve.

The features of a structured management method can be summarised by a few basic facts:

- it brings together many standard procedures and techniques,

- provides a standard for management which can be applied to all types and sizes of a project,

- can be adapted to suit deferring projects, existing procedures and cultural attitudes,

- a quality approach to project management.

A structured management method provides management with the ability to react swiftly and efficiently to business and strategy changes, to understand what projects and studies are in hand and their interrelationships both, with each other and with the overall strategy. It, also, provides an effective way of controlling costs and resources at the business level.

All management methods demand the participation of senior management in any type of project; from the initial stage to the phase where a completed system is handed over to the user community. A project, also, needs the involvement of quality assurance and other support staff, where all the participants form the steering committee and the support groups.

The committee and all participating follow a project management method, comprising integrated procedures, based on a number of principles and documented in a set of procedural manuals.

The principles are:

- organisation,
- planning,
- controls,
- stages,
- product based approach,
- quality.

The overall objective of the structured management method is to enable the right people to make the right decision at the right time. This formally enforces the involvement and commitment of the business, users, and technical interest in a project.

It creates a flexible organisational hierarchy of:

- people representing business and users,
- project manager, responsible to the committee for day to day management,
- project team members,
- people providing support and assuring delivery of quality products.

Plans are the basis of the management of any project. They provide the benchmark of information required for decision making, controlling, communicating, and reporting.

Plans at each level address:

- scope,
- products,
- quality,
- risk management,

- timescale,
- resources,
- costs,
- controls.

Project control is carried out at two levels, by:

- formal assessment meetings,
- the project manager at checkpoint meetings.

The objectives of each meeting are defined and guidance is provided on the agenda and procedures. In certain projects, it is recognised that there may be a requirement to control the work of the project in more detail.

Project management methods are concentrating on the things to be produced, rather than the activities required to produce them. These things are called products and the approach ensures that all products are identified and clearly defined before proceeding with activity planning. It is a significant aid to better estimating and planning.

A structured management method, also, provides detailed guidance on the procedures and techniques required to apply the principles.

These procedures and techniques include:

- project initiation,
- product planning techniques,
- business case,
- quality review,
- configuration management,
- change control,
- documentation.

The application of the procedures and techniques is flexible and it is this aspect which makes a management method practical and successful.

A project management system should be utilised on all sizeable projects undertaken. A Project Manager should be appointed, responsible for the agreement and delivery of project products to agreed deadlines throughout the project's lifecycle.

The main project management issues include:

- proper user, staff and management training,
- management commitment,
- budgets,
- user and expert time,
- identify key users,
- schedule time for analysis and design,
- establish metrics,
- small teams,
- testing implementation and handover to users.

The Project Manager should produce a weekly status report which will be provided one day prior to a weekly progress meeting.

This report will have the following format:

- milestones, summary report of the current and previous status of milestones,
- progress, a narrative of progress.
- changes to the project baseline, including change notices,
- issues, details reported for current week and the status of those previously reported,
- variances in either time, or effort for any milestone,

- resource usage for the week,

- external factors that may impact upon progress, but not within the control of the project management,

- cost reports of any costs incurred during the week, excluding resource costs and known regular costs,

- objectives and risks for the next period,

- recommendations and issues for discussion.

The weekly meeting should take place between:

- the user Project Manager, or representative,

- the system Project Manager, or representative.

During the project lifecycle, project issues can occur which require analysis, documentation and resolutions.

Project issues fall into those that occur during the:

- development and delivery of the system,

- operational life of the system.

Any change to the requirements, or to any document once it has been formally agreed, is subject to the following change control procedures:

- a change control notice will be raised by the user requesting the change,

- an estimate of the impact of the change on the schedule and costing of the project will be prepared by the system Project Manager,

- the change details will be transmitted to the users representative for authorisation,

- if the change is authorised, then the change control notice will be annotated by the member of the project team, who implements the change to indicate that it has been completed. A copy will then be filed with the documentation affected,

- the documentation itself will be updated to reflect the change, with update pages sent to all nominated parties,

- all changes during the project, whether by the user, or system developer will be controlled by the IT project area.

Throughout the life of the project, reviews of critical documents are necessary. The procedures for review of these documents are as follows:

- all critical documents will be reviewed within the project team structure to ensure adherence to the project standards,

- the quality to be randomly selected and reviewed by the Assurance Manager,

In case of controlled documents, this will include a check that the documents have the following details:

- document identification,

- document name,

- name of system Project Manager,

- distribution list,

- current version.

The strategy of the system acceptance will be defined by the user. The subsequent plan and test scripts will be based upon the standards. As part of a quality management system, a senior manager undertakes the auditing of the project. The quality auditor operates outside the design and builds team structures.

Before delivery of the system, a training schedule for the users will be agreed. Additionally, prior to any handing over, the system will be tested and should any problems arise, these will be reported and remedied before the users sign off.

With the state-of-the-art in commercial computing, the accelerated progress in technology and the demand made on more systems development, the IT management find themselves increasingly occupied in the selection of larger number of specialised staff. Such is the great weight on IT managers, to fulfil new job responsibilities and to replace those who leave for greener pastures.

The vacancies for system engineers are constantly increasing, at such a rate that a new industry has developed. Additional to the traditional recruitment, the demand for the supply of contractors, mainly for systems analysis and programming, has increased in proportions. Agencies for freelancers are now deeply rooted as a service to IT.

The contracting analysts/programmers are in their thousands and agencies in their hundreds. The cost to the organisation for such a service is huge, often enough remuneration paid being higher than what the business directors are paid. Frequently more than the IT manager gets. With such numbers of candidates involved and an unknown expertise at that, the systems managers are faced with the additional responsibility of frequent interviews and uncertainty as to what kind of know-how they will obtain from contractors.

The agencies do not have the knowledge to scrutinise every system engineer on their registers. It is a well known fact that the agents submit the CVs of individuals without even checking on the contractor's experience. The agencies arrange for the interviews between the company's managers and the freelancers over the telephone. For this kind of service the agencies receive between 20% and 40% of the contracting fees. The larger, established contracting agencies have a firm charge of 33% commission.

The IT management and their staff are faced with the overload of interviews. It is an under-estimated task. With all the pressures from within the systems areas, it is a wonder how systems can be developed and become operational within the quoted timescales and costs.

As an example, using the two extremes of the systems engineering professions of Analysts and Programmers, it is of paramount importance to use the right techniques for interviewing systems staff. In hiring systems engineers, it must be remembered that an analyst is the person who keeps in touch with the users and the programmer is the one that builds the system.

The analyst must be an out-going person, a good mixer; a person who can get on with other people, easily collect details and must be a good systems representative. As the psychometrics expert will declare - the psychological personality type of an extrovert thinker.

On the other extreme, bear in mind that the programmer has to decipher the documents the analyst produces, in order to start constructing the required system. This makes the programmer the psychological personality of an introvert sensation type.

There are many other types of professionals within systems engineering; designers, database administrators, operators, strategists, and a few more. In interviewing, therefore, the interviewer will be helped enormously if he/she makes a few notes beforehand regarding the type of person needed to fill in the responsibilities within the systems professions.

In interviewing, handing out a short narrative and asking the interviewee to turn it into diagrams and programming coding is not on. The candidate must be relaxed, made to feel wanted, important and then prompted to expand on items relevant to the vacancy.

A system designing is such a modern profession, its responsibilities and qualities are hardly known to psychologists, psychometrists, and professional recruiters. For instance, one cannot rely on aptitude testing alone, as there are no set rules. Experience in systems areas and knowing what is needed is the best guide and basis for the interview.

Within the various scales of recruitment are the newcomers to the professions of systems management. These are the graduates of IT 'hybrid' management courses, and the MBAs whose degree material is based on traditional management. Commercial computing demands organisational experience gained within business functions relating to systems.

The young graduates of the first degree education can be recruited with the proviso that they get trained within the systems business parameters. It is true that the new universities in their computing sciences subjects cover methodologies, databases and programming, but the question still prevails, as to whether the extend of commercial experience embedded in the lecturers and their tutorials and those running the academic departments is sufficient. Let it be stressed that this statement refers to the business computing and systems development in the commercial world.

Universities have progressed enormously in their research on artificial intelligence and other fields such as parallelism. The outside world still runs systems on mainframes and applications as required by the users. The modern construction of business systems and tools developed, suit the personalities and the abilities of those who use these applications.

Faced with such problems, the IT management pays a lot of attention to interviewing. After all, like any other recruitment, employing a human being (permanent or contractor) is still a big investment of time, costs, and other resources.

It must be added, that the interviewing techniques in commercial computing are applied to applicants for vacant positions, as well as the users who ask for new systems, the repairing of an existing one, or the extraction of the data based information.

Interviewing is the most commonly used way of acquiring basic concepts and requirements from the users. It is an activity that needs careful planning and execution. It is crucial to plan an interview to ensure that it is as productive as possible.

Whether interviewing an applicant for a vacancy, or a user for his/her requirements, it is worthwhile bearing the following in mind:

- ensure that the interviewee is prepared for the interview,
- notify the subject to be covered,
- the time and location of the interview,
- probable length of the interview,
- ensure that a room is ready, away from the interviewee's workplace, thus minimising distractions,
- make the interviewee comfortable with the computing terminology and jargon,
- build a rapport, listen and show interest.

As an interviewer, practise the art of relaxation on you and then apply the technique to the candidate. Remember that the users' interviewees may offer details on what they think you want to know. A good analyst will steer the discussion to the domain of interest, whereas a job applicant will be nervous, anxious and feel as if on the receiving end.

Businesses have problems which they need to solve. They, also, have requirements which altogether enable the smooth running of their environment. To establish the appropriate running of the business organisation, projects need to be set.

An organisation is probably undergoing significant change. Changes span functional boundaries, case conflict, and concern and present a major risk to the business and those managers responsible for the development of systems. Many companies are now adopting a project-based approach to managing the change of systems and their development.

Managers of today and of the future, require skills in managing projects. These skills are supplementary to the line management skills. A company needs to enhance business planning and control structures to explicitly link system implementation to business led projects and programmes.

A project in information technology is a temporary situation within the working groups (the system users) and the computing management, with the objective of delivering a product. The resulting product relies on the project progress and how it is approached in its scope to deliver.

For a project to be successful it needs:

- management at all levels,
- team building and staff motivation,
- planning and controls,
- quality standards to follow,
- communication between users and management,
- objectives and scope,
- adequate skills and experienced resources,
- explicit documentation and training.

Unlike existing systems operational management, where one deals with established computer services, project management encounters the unfamiliar, new problems and needs for change.

In managing a project, a list of activities will not be enough. The project must be product-based. A methodology needs to be followed, procedures to be applied. The appropriate procedures, therefore, give the advantage of common standards being applied to the management of all projects, with directional emphasis to meeting the corporate objectives.

Always remembering that a system is built with quality and that the application of the procedures and techniques must be flexible and practical:

- for the users,
- to fulfil a process,
- benefit the business function.

Project management supports the implementation of the business strategies with explicit link to the development plan. This provides management with the ability to react swiftly and efficiently to any changes, to understand the project stages and steps in hand and their relationship with each other. It, also, provides an effective way of controlling costs and resources at all levels.

The appropriate analysis and design methodology will assist the project team members to concentrate on the system components to be produced. It enables the management and the analysts to identify and clearly define all the development phases. It is, also, a significant contributor to quality, better estimating, and planning.

This means that a systems manager and his/her team members need to establish project control standards, which will specifically include:

1. purpose,
2. scope,
3. input,
4. planning,
5. progress control.

1. Purpose:

The purpose of the project control standards is to define the standard to be used within system development for managing the project in terms of project planning and progress control. The objectives of project management being:

- establish clear objectives and scope for a project,

- ensure roles and responsibilities are well defined and understood,

- break work down into schedules and deliverables,

- plan how an individual project will achieve the implementation of the required end product within a progressively refined and agreed schedule and budget.

A project control framework is necessary within which project management skills and techniques are exercised.

2. Scope:

This standard addresses Project Control in a new system development environment, i.e. a multi-team situation with Team Leaders and an overall Project Manager.

It covers the planning of each phase for each team and its members and the progressing of those plans.

3. Input:

The inputs will vary with the size and stage of development:

- Terms of Reference (ToR, for a new project) and Project Initiation Document (PID),

- key documentation from earlier phases (for an existing project)

- procedures manual

4. Planning:

The following steps describe a team leader's project control, carried out at the start of a project, or when rescheduling (as a result of supplying more tasks, or changing estimates).

- Task Identification. A source of information for this will be the overall project plan and the activities listed.

- Estimating. Estimating for project control planning is carried out using the bottom-up approach, starting with the steps involved, and building upwards. When all tasks have been identified and estimated, an overall schedule can be drawn, which accounts for resource constraints, deadlines and overheads.

• **Scheduling.** The basics of scheduling are to take the information from task identification, sizing, and resource allocation and to build a schedule which meets the necessary timescales.

5 Progress Control:

The Project Control system and progress meetings are the principal mechanisms for monitoring and controlling the progress of a project.

• **Progress Meetings.** Aside from the informal contact maintained between a team leader and team members, each person should receive a regular progress meeting, on a one-to-one basis. Also, each team leader should meet with the project manager on a similar basis.

• **Team Meetings.** A regular weekly meeting of all team members is important, in order to maintain communication and to resolve issues where input is required.

• **Outstanding Issues.** As projects progress, design issues may emerge which require a solution. At the end of the development, any loose ends not resolved can be passed to the support team for future enhancements to the system.

• **Rescheduling.** Even the best planned project may have its scope changed by changes in requirements, or late design changes. Changes of this type can cause disruption which outweighs the benefits they provide, so it is important to keep them to a minimum.

7. SYSTEMS DEVELOPMENT PROCEDURES

The system specification procedures form the basis within the conventional business environment for setting out the standards for system development. They describe a step by step approach to developing and implementing computer systems. They define the documents to be produced, the controls to be applied and the tasks to be performed.

The intention is that these procedures be applied flexibly. On the other hand, the phases are designed for sequential development, with the output from one phase being the input to the next, all leading to the eventual implementation of the system. Project plans should be drawn up to suit the particular project and then adhered to.

The procedures define the paths that will be followed in projects set up to develop computer systems. A project is, thus, described in terms of its major divisions (Phases), its Control Points, the Activities that are accomplished in each phase, and the Tasks that go to make up those activities.

A project starts with an initiation and ends with a review and user training. The Project Initiation Document (PID) will incite the feasibility study and the terms of reference. The review will include the report to the users and the appropriate steps for the system training and the training manual distributed to all the users involved in the running of the system-to-be.

Otherwise, the project has the following phases:

1. Business Analysis: Users' business Problems and Requirements and the initial top level Dataflow Diagram.

2. Systems Analysis: System Proposal, Functional Decomposition, Dataflow Diagram, Logical Data Structure and Process Descriptions,

3. Design Options: Technical Design Options,

4. Functional Analysis: Process Model, Detailed Dataflow Diagram and Process Descriptions,

5. Data Analysis: Data Model, Entity Life History,

6. Physical Design/Build, System Specification, Program Code.

The system development lifecycle, in outlining the activities to be followed and the tasks to be carried out in a project, provides the framework for planning and defining a project.

The development lifecycle does not ensure that projects will meet a particular level of quality, nor does it ensure that work carried out will be both, efficient and effective. That is a matter of how people perform and it is the goal of project management to make sure that conditions exist for them to be efficient and effective.

The framework of the lifecycle with its different phases, offers some guidance on when project management should be applied. Each phase has a beginning, middle, and end. Project management procedures are ongoing and required to fit in with the dimensions of the workday and reporting cycles.

Project management is a series of activities that are carried out during a project by the leader:

- planning,
- estimating,
- monitoring,
- reporting,
- quality control,
- resource allocation,
- communication.

The performance of any computer department can only be judged by the service given to the system users. This clearly means change in business through projects. It involves people and the experience they carry with them; experience in system building when a company needs it most, when this type of people, the best in the organisation are in short supply and great demand. They are usually, therefore, not available when needed for a critical new project - to develop the long awaited system.

The System Specification starts as far back as Systems Analysis and is completed when programming begins. A standard is required for conducting systems design because a uniform approach is needed across all projects to ensure understanding and consistency.

The standard outputs are required as input to programming activities. The systems specifications, therefore, need to be written in a rigorous and consistent manner to ensure that all user requirements are catered for and all business processing is completely and accurately defined and documented.

The following may be input to system specification:

- current, systems documentation and specifications,
- user requirements documentation and proposals,
- system proposal from system analysis phase,
- process descriptions, dataflow diagrams and layouts from the functional analysis phase,
- minutes of meetings with users.

The System Specification is the phase where the lowest level dataflow diagrams and descriptions from process analysis are pulled together.

The aim of the process analysis is to reach a detailed logical design sufficient for all specification work. A standard is required for conducting process analysis because a uniform approach is needed across all projects. It concentrates on processes rather than data. Thorough process analysis encourages understanding of the system and user environment. The outputs from the process analysis are required for the system design processes.

There can be many inputs into process analysis depending on the nature and complexity of the project.

The following may be input to process analysis:

- systems documentation and specifications from the current system,
- user requirements and proposals,
- decomposition of dataflow diagrams.

The dataflow diagram is a powerful input to design because it identifies the data flows, data stores and processing involved. The technique is top-down; an overview followed by increasingly lower levels of detail.

This is then followed by a full system review. The purpose of a review is to define the process for understanding what is needed and as means of checking the quality of work throughout the systems development lifecycle.

The objectives of holding a review of a piece of work are to:

- ensure the work meets its requirements,
- trap errors as early as possible,
- provide a focus on outstanding issues which lie in the pathway to completion of a given task,
- check adherence to standards.

It is clear that in practice it would not be appropriate to subject all outputs to the same level of review and several variants of the review process are required.

The different levels of review allow for the:

- importance of the review material,
- authority of the attendees,
- level at which the review is documented,

- formality with which the review is held.

Then the physical design follows the review. The physical design converts the results of process and data design into an implementable computer solution and defines the computer/clerical interface. This is evaluated against the requirements and amended as appropriate.

The scope of the physical design is to cover the technical design of application systems. It concentrates on the design of the system processes, rather than the design of databases.

The following may be input to systems design:

- current systems documentation and specifications,
- user requirements and solutions,
- system proposal from analysis phase,
- process descriptions, dataflow diagrams and layouts from functional analysis phase.

Requirements often change during the design phase and new ones emerge. In addition, it often raises more questions requiring further analysis. Therefore, the final design may only be arrived at through several iterations of logical and physical design.

In every review the Quick Dataflow Diagramming becomes extremely useful.

Dataflow diagrams (DFDs) are used for process analysis, to show the logical:

- system processes, hierarchy and their relationships,
- datastores, the system's data 'at rest',
- data flows, the system's data 'in motion' between two processes, or between a process and a datastore.

To present a complete system description, additional documentation is necessary for each flow, each datastore, and each process.

It is the DFD which structures the analysis process and drawing the DFD helps the Analyst to:

- deal with the information collected during data gathering, in an orderly manner,

- avoid being overwhelmed by detail and losing sight of the overall picture,

- document the proposed system in a convenient format as input to design,

- communicate with users.

In diagramming, the following conventions apply to drawing dataflow diagrams:

- **External Entity**, usually represented by a circle outside the boundary. This is the source, or destination of data outside the area under study. If the circle has a line across the corner, then the external entity is used elsewhere and has been duplicated for diagramming convenience.

- **Data Flow**, depicted by an arrow and a description put alongside the arrow. The arrow shows direction of flow. Flows are labelled with a meaningful name describing content of the flow, not the document or report carrying the data.

- **Process**, usually represented by a rectangle, it can be a manual process or computerised. Processes are labelled with an appropriate and clear-cut name, which should be a verb followed by an object phrase. A process 'box' should be labelled for easy reference. This should reflect the top-down hierarchy. (Process: 1, 1.1, 1.1.1/1.1.2/1.1.3, Process: 2, etc.)

- **Datastore**, symbolised by an open-ended rectangle. A name for the datastore that is meaningful to users is written inside the symbol. Datastores should be numbered sequentially and prefixed by the letter 'D'.

In drawing a DFD the following must always be considered:

- The highest level picture of the system is called a 'context diagram' and consists of one box representing the system under study.

- External Entities are shown outside the boundary line, along with the flows between the study system and the externals.

- Having agreed a context diagram with the user management, a first level DFD is created containing high level functions.

- The functions on the first level DFD are then exploded by creating another DFD for each particular process. Each further level clarifies the activities within a system and shows an increasing level of detail in the activities themselves and the dataflows that connect them.

- In a new system partitioning should go to the level where each process box corresponds to a specific process. Partitioning is an iterative process. It takes several reviews to get to a perfect diagram.

- With partitioning it is always difficult to know when a sufficient level of detail has been reached.

The following guidelines may help:

- More than five flows into a process may indicate that the activity is over complex, although up to seven may be accommodated. Less than three, may indicate insufficient information.

- The narrative description should not take more than a couple of pages.

- The process should relate to units of work recognised by the user.

- Generally, it should be possible to identify a single input that drives the process.

- Often, there is only one major output.

- DFDs should be kept as simple as possible to avoid confusion. A good rule of thumb is no more than seven processes per page. If there are more than this, it probably means that there are more details than necessary. To be on the safe side, create another level by exploding one process into a lower level DFD.

- Symbols should be duplicated on the diagram to avoid crossing lines. A duplicate should be marked with a line on the left hand side of the symbol.

- Avoid partitioning according to company organisation, as the diagrams show functions not organisations.

Before they are coded, programs need to be designed. There needs to be a structure which shows how and where the processes diagrammed in the DFD and described in the System Specification are to be performed.

Structured English is used to represent the design. This is a simplified form of English, presented in defined manner. Within the structure so formed, normal English is used, although in as succinct a form as possible.

The relevant systems specification proceeds to a program design ready for coding. To enable this, the following inputs are necessary:

- decomposition diagram,
- DFDs at the program or transaction level,
- system specification,
- system flowchart,
- data structure diagram.

A program design which is structured is easier to maintain and understand. The structuring of the design means principally that the design should be driven by the flows of input and output data.

The program designer or programmer should arrange for regular program and code Walkthroughs with another programmer/designer. The walkthrough session should check:

- adherence to programming standards,

- that the code matches the design structure,

- that the code performs the processing defined in the system specification,

- that database accessing is correct.

Program designing and programming in general, requires disciplined management since this needs clearly defined objectives to fulfil the overall project.

Project management must, therefore, ensure that the investment of resources, time, and effort are fully justified and fulfilled. This includes program definition and the setting up of efficient structures. Whatever the requirements, experience is of major importance in helping and controlling programming.

8. CASE TOOLS AND METHODOLOGIES

As organisations strive to increase productivity, to reduce costs, to shorten cycle times, to improve product and service quality, so the demands made on systems for modifications and for new information increase. Being able to make better decisions based on quality information and having the flexibility to respond to new opportunities increasingly, depends on having the right systems in place at the right time.

Applications developed based on older technologies may well not meet current requirements in some or many areas, such as:

- functionality,
- ease of use,
- data access,
- maintainability,
- flexibility,
- robustness,
- costs.

With the wide range of application environments and building blocks now available, it is still possible to have an affordable system designed and built to meet specific business requirements. This gives the flexibility and control to define the system the way the users want it and then to change and adapt the system to support the business over coming years.

Computer-aided Software Engineering (CASE) tools address the application design stage. For business systems they can be extremely useful to assist in the design of both, the application and the data structure.

Rapid Application Development (RAD) techniques incorporate a series of steps which business people and Information Technology professionals work through together to develop a prototype of the application representing the business process before full scale development.

The objectives of analysis is to understand what a particular area of the business does and how information is exchanged, created and modified by business processes.

With a clear understanding of the information needs of a business area, the system engineer can determine which business activities to automate and then develop those systems so they meet end user requirements.

The design helps users move from a logical representation of 'what' a given system is to perform, into the physical specifications for 'how' the system will actually be implemented.

In order to handle the complex nature of a system, it is often helpful to break down the processes and data of the system into manageable pieces. Decomposition diagrams are an easy way to partition the data and process requirements of the system, by analysing and application, refining high level business processes into lower level processes. These processes can then be broken down further until the analyst reaches a level of detail where a process can best be described in terms of its procedural logic.

The decomposition diagram helps to create and maintain diagrams for:

• process decomposition; depict the analysis of processes into sub-processes,

• data decomposition; show how general groupings of data break down into more specific data entities,

• organisational decomposition; describe the hierarchical structure of the organisation.

The analysis stage is unique in its approach to integrating the process model with the data model. The analyst can build the application data model by defining, one at a time, the data model for each individual process.

Dataflow diagrams can help describe how a business area or system functions. They show how data flows into and out of the business area or system, how processes transform data and the external agents (recipients/sources) that interface with the system.

Entities are the subjects of information (people, places, things) about which a business needs to keep data. An entity diagram provides a graphic way of describing the data requirements of a system and how they interrelate. The entity diagram, also, helps describe and characterise the relationships among these entities.

In many Information Technology (IT) departments, the complexity of applications often dictates that development responsibilities be divided among members of a project team. The ability to share information is a fundamental requirement for systems development tools.

Such tools, Computer-aided Software Engineer (CASE - some system engineers describe them as 'System', instead of 'Software') tools are designed to offer unequalled flexibility in combining and reconciling the work of multiple users. The analyst can selectively consolidate and separate, either whole, or partial encyclopaedias, or selected objects and maintain multiple encyclopaedias for different projects or users.

9. INFORMATION SYSTEMS EXPLAINED

It is hard to imagine business today without information systems. Information Technology in general is an important part of business and everyday life. It has become very important for individuals and organisations, in the ability to compete, perform and prosper.

As a support structure and as a tool for business, systems can deliver a number of significant benefits. Costs can be reduced, productivity increased, services improved and profits enhanced.

People at the sharp end of business; want a better understanding of the way that systems are developed and function. It is hoped that in this book systems issues are explained and that computing helps people to comprehend the broad aspects of technologies available to assist in achieving personal and business objectives.

Systems ought to be about enabling business and personal change.

In explaining Commerce and the Internet, the term 'Electronic Commerce' is commonly used to mean doing business electronically. It is the paperless exchange of critical business information between companies and their suppliers, government departments, financial institutions, customers and companies, even within organisations.

Businesses today see the electronic commerce as a way to streamline operations, reach new markets, and serve their clients more efficiently. It can often be a catalyst for business change through business process re-engineering. A streamlined new process nearly always entails some degree of automation. Since many business processes cut across boundaries between departments, divisions and even companies, electronic commerce is a natural way to automate these processes.

A popular method of communication for exchanging data is Electronic Data Interchange (EDI). EDI may be defined as the 'exchange of standardised structured information between computer systems'.

EDI lends itself to the exchange of high volumes of information in a fixed format agreed by industry groups. This includes invoicing and payments, retail point-of-sale, bank transactions and manufacturing inventories. Because information is created and transferred electronically, there is no need for paperwork. This eliminated the need for re-keying data, which saves labour, speeds up processes and reduces details errors. Significant cost savings and reduced lead times can be achieved.

Processes can be automated and re-structured so that maximum operational efficiency is obtained. EDI operates by direct connection between users and over private and public data networks, ensuring privacy and security. As it uses highly structured formats, transmission speeds can be increased and overall costs reduced.

An electronic commerce business solution relies on a network to act as a conduit for the transfer of data. Often, a 'value-added network' from a commercial provider is used, to provide the infrastructure required to transfer data securely and reliably among trading partners.

One of the ideas brought forward, is whether the Internet will replace these value-added network services. The Internet is one methods of exchanging business data, but not the only means. A commercial network eliminates many of the technical matching issues and provides services not available on the Internet, such as security, tracking, and audit ability. The Internet is an important element of an electronic commerce solution, but is not the only one.

Until a few years ago, the Internet was not well known. One could scarcely have predicted the impact it would have on the world of systems and computers communications.

From its inception in the 1960s, the Internet evolved into a global network of business, academic and government computers. In recent years, businesses and individual users have recognised its potential as a way of communicating; by exchanging electronic mail, transferring files, accessing information services and communicating via bulletin boards and computer conferencing.

The communication has been accompanied by the emergence of a part of the Internet known as the World Wide Web, which allows information to be presented in a graphical format; incorporating text, images, video and sound.

Any user with a suitable personal computer can access the Web through a connection to the Internet using the normal telephone line and view information using low cost software tools, known as browsers.

Businesses are now setting up electronic shop-fronts and information sites on the World Wide Web and starting to realise the immense potential for reaching a global audience.

However, this open access to the vast storehouse of information raises a number of issues. The openness of the Internet leads to concerns over security. The Internet is a public set of networks that interconnect and are not inherently secure. As a consequence, there is a demand for effective software security tools known as 'firewalls'. These act as a secure gateway to limit outsiders' access to a company's data systems and provide control over staff access to the Internet.

Companies and individuals are reluctant to transmit and exchange sensitive details over the Internet, such as credit card information. The problem is now being addressed by developing effective encryption tools. The combination of firewalls and encryption will enable the realisation of the Internet's full commercial potential.

One genuine limiting factor on Internet usage is data transmission speeds. Although these have improved in recent years, for most users they remain painfully slow. It takes a few minutes to download and read even a basic Web page. Transferring large data files is often impracticably slow. These and other management issues associated with security, training and implementation, should be taken into account when considering the Internet as part of a business strategy.

Over the years, the word was that the mainframe computer was on the way out. The growth of the personal computers on the desk-top was claimed to replace the mainframe as the preferred business information technology platform, well before the end of the century.

The reports of the mainframe's death have turned out to be greatly exaggerated. The fact that mainframes have been around for so long helps explain why companies still use them.

Historically, data has been safe and secure on a mainframe. The cost and benefits of moving it to another type of system are difficult to justify. The longevity of the mainframe means that it is a mature environment as far as security, structure and disciplined operational processes are concerned. Innovations in computing may appear to be more sophisticated, but lack the tools to deliver the integrity, security and availability of data required to run critical business systems.

Mainframes are still perceived to be the best place for sensitive information and for running data intensive centralised systems, such as personnel, payroll, accounts, and inventories.

In modern computing environments, the mainframe assumes a new role. Additional to its running of large systems, it is becoming a large-scale data server. Companies recognise the need to provide centralised management and protection for critical data distributed throughout the organisation. In fact, the amount of data storage on the mainframe is growing and so is the data held on systems elsewhere. This gives the systems function the added responsibility of storing, organising, managing and distributing the data.

The concept of managing data across an organisation requires the facility to manage its storage in a uniform manner, implementing consistent policies and standards and enforcing the protection of critical data. This is achieved via the use of software tools, which offer an overall view of the data stored.

The concept of storage management is well established in the mainframe environment and has been the basis for the replication of those disciplines across the business enterprise, leading to more efficient use of resources, greater ease of management and security of information.

Desk-top personal computers have become extensively used alongside mainframes. The emergence of the PC led to a different perception of computing. Users expect systems which are easy to build, operate and use, with highly graphical and intuitive screens. These facilities have not been a strength of the mainframe in the past.

Many organisations have rationalised a requirement for centralised control with the need for end user autonomy by creating links and networks, utilising the strengths of both mainframes and personal computers. In effect, the mainframe is used to collect, store and process business information from a variety of sources, with individuals and work groups then accessing the centralised data using PCs.

Software houses have risen to this challenge by developing a range of software tools which allow PC users to access and analyse mainframe data and integrate it with desktop systems, such as spreadsheets, word processors and other business software tools. They need to be able to locate relevant information easily, using everyday PC language rather than specialised computer commands and are not interested in where the information lies and how it is retrieved.

The users expect to be able to search all available data sources in one go without worrying about the different structures and systems used by the various databases they are searching. Alternatively, links can be created between the PC and mainframe applications enabling automatic update of desktop data whenever the source is changed on the mainframe.

The longevity of the mainframe means that the management of services it provides to the business is well understood and consequently more controllable. The mainframe acts as a hub, linked to many other areas of the organisation's systems and provides a central viewpoint for ensuring that users have systems up and running when they need them.

Consequently, a range of tools to manage the operational side of providing these services has evolved. These allow a high degree of automation and relate the services to their importance to the business. Hence, if a part of the system, or network fails, the services which are most critical to the running of the business can be addressed first, whilst less critical services assume a lower priority. In today's business environment, when organisations trade round the clock, management of systems to this sophistication is vital to business success. This type of service simply cannot be managed without the control available with mainframe systems.

The mainframe plays an important part of the evolution of an organisation's systems and often provides the most logical platform to run business systems effectively. If the mainframe did ever die, it has certainly risen again.

A client/server system is a 'modular' approach to computer systems. Instead of all aspects of the system being held in one place, a server holds applications and data which can be accessed from a number of 'clients' who have their own processing capability.

In the most advanced systems, any computer on the network could act as a server for some applications and as a client for others. This is significantly different to the conventional local area network (LAN), where typically one computer will control the network and hold data, although applications tend to be held on each PC or workstation.

Client/server systems were conceived when the personal computer emerged as a credible platform for business systems. Users became accustomed to powerful desk-top applications and the ease of use provided by graphical user interfaces, such as Windows and OS/2. By linking these computers, it was reasoned, mainframe-based business systems could be replaced with groups of computers which were collectively as powerful, but individually easier and more flexible to use.

The new-style systems support greater integration and collaboration between corporate-wide and single user desk-top applications. Employees at all levels of an organisation have access to a company's systems, but do not need the support and training associated with traditional text-based programs. This wider use of graphical interfaces across the enterprise has enabled the implementation of better reporting tools and more flexible access to data through sophisticated information systems.

One of the reasons for the evolution of the client/server philosophy was the growth of power on the desk-top, via the personal computer. However, organisations soon realised that a huge amount of data resided elsewhere in the business, often collected and collated over many years and held in a secure and controlled environment, such as mainframe computers.

There seemed to be little reason to migrate or relocate these systems on to a different type of computer, especially if the underlying business processes they would support were to remain fundamentally the same.

For this reason, the client/server concept encompasses all sizes of computers and not just the PC. However, a business structures its systems and data, the most important business benefit to be delivered is increased ease of use and flexibility of data access. Often, the best returns on investment in client/server have been achieved when personal computers have provided an interface with existing systems, but with the retention of the underlying programs and processes.

When implementing client/server systems, organisations can, therefore, choose between developing simple graphical interfaces to enable a personal computer to access mainframe data, or they may decide on a totally new application built from scratch. In each case, effective software tools are needed to develop the new interfaces and support the integration of new and old systems.

Software tools are available which cover virtually every aspect of building and implementing client/server systems. The best are easy to use, typically running on PCs. Structurally incorporating rapid application development concepts and processes which involve the input of business users into the building of effective systems to support business needs. Usually, tools of varying kinds are required to make the most of computing elements already in existence.

Systems re-engineering software enables existing mainframe applications to be transferred to other computer types without losing the original investment in programming. Connectivity tools and terminal emulation software enable computers to access information on different platforms. Graphical development tools assist users to create new screen layouts and applications. Alternatively, fast productivity gains can be achieved from the use of integrating software, which takes older-style, text-based applications and creates an easy to use graphical screen for the user. Not only is this easier to use and, therefore, more productive, but it means that a number of applications can be combined on the desk-top.

Users of the systems need access to data wherever it is located, without having to be concerned with where it is, or techniques of accessing it. Sophisticated software tools are available to locate data stored in multiple locations and to allow it to be extracted in a common format for compilation of reports and integration into other applications.

It would be true to say that, in many organisations, client/server is happening despite IT and not because of it. The amount of technology and skill accumulating on the desk-top is growing exponentially, as is the need to connect to shared resources such as databases and mail services. A move to client/server should deliver concrete business advantages, integrating the PC and the corporate mainframe, thus increasing flexibility.

Such corporate integration leads to more direct business involvement in the use of information technology. However, there is often increased cost associated with client/server over a traditional centralised computing structure. A complete realignment of the IT function is needed to provide managed support to the distributed systems which are now running the business.

Most organisations have an inherited legacy of systems. These inherited systems will have been in operation for a number of years, on mainframes and running bespoke systems which were written in house, or by a contracting consultant. At first sight, legacy systems appear to have limited use in a modern organisation, with the exception of one very important fact. Their longevity means they hold a huge amount of vital, critical data. The business processes which they support, have been developed over the years and investment made in getting the systems right.

With the industry hype on the demise of the mainframe, organisations started to wonder whether the mainframe and the legacy systems running on it were declining and whether they should be replaced with new workstation and client/server systems. However, reality shows that this vast change is not easily achieved, that companies still depend upon legacy systems for the vast majority of their operations and that new systems continue to be built for the mainframe.

It has transpired that most of the conflict between the new client/server technologies and legacy applications is based on misconceptions. Companies can gain significant advantages by incorporating new features into legacy systems. Re-use of legacy code significantly reduces cost and risk, while spending the time taken to deliver new business systems.

Sophisticated software tools enable IT departments to inspect, assess, document and record their legacy applications scientifically and objectively. Further tools can then be used, if required, to extract the best of the application code and provide the basis for migration to new developments.

Since legacy systems may have been constantly developed over the years, it is also important to use the relevant software tools to re-document their structure, to ensure that they can be supported and maintained. This ensures that the vital business processes they support are not threatened.

One current issue requiring this attention is the 'Year 2000' issue. Many legacy systems were envisaged to have a short life and needed to minimise the use of computer storage which was relatively expensive in the early days of systems building. These systems were written to hold only last two digits of the year in the date field and have endured and played a vital role in running the business.

It is now necessary to use appropriate software tools to identify all occurrences of 2-digit fields and change them to 4-digit, otherwise systems will assume that the date is reset to

1900, when the new millennium is reached. An example of this would be a financial loan application, which would mature before it started interest due would be impossible to calculate and chaos would rein.

The typical computer user today needs to access and use information throughout the organisation to produce business plans, reports, and presentations. The users need to draw information from a variety of sources to help them make the sort of high quality informed decisions that give their business competitive edge, greater efficiency and improved productivity.

Many organisations have realised that their legacy systems can have a prolonged life if the information they hold can be made available to this new type of user. For this reason, legacy systems are often incorporated into client/server systems, where PC users have direct, but controlled access to mainframe data.

In these situations the mainframe is used as a secure gateway to corporate mission-critical systems and as a centralised repository for enterprise data. As an example, retailers and financial institutions are continuing to use legacy systems to control most of their on-line transactions for hole-in-the-wall cash machines, or electronic point-of-sale data collection and processing.

With this new understanding of legacy systems and the tools that now exist to leverage their potential, their future is assured. Legacy systems can be integrated effectively with new systems, so that the data they hold and business functions they support are available throughout the enterprise. This not only prolongs their cost-effective life but also reduces costs through minimising the need to acquire new skills and purchase new hardware, software, and infrastructure.

10. Re-engineering

Business Process Re-engineering (BPR) is the strategic application of analysis and change at a departmental or corporate level to deliver business benefits such as cost savings and efficiency gains. Information technology is often applied to BPR projects, but it is not in itself the BPR. It is more accurately the method enabling business change.

Effective re-engineering starts with assessing operations at a corporate, departmental, or even functional level. Each of the business processes involved is analysed to see how it works, how it interrelates with other processes, what it achieves, and what it costs. The next stage is to investigate whether each process is necessary and how it might be improved. Finally, new processes are developed and implemented so that improvements are made to overall efficiency, with reduced costs and increased productivity. All of this can be achieved without any information technology whatsoever.

However, in most organisations it is likely that IT can be used to help automate certain processes, eliminate others and introduce new ways of working. For these reasons, it is closely associated with re-engineering and the allied area of workflow, which addresses the need to improve the management of the passage of information through an organisation. Software modelling tools can also aid the process of documenting business work flows in order that the processes are comprehensively understood before considering change.

The key benefits of the business process re-engineering are typically the elimination of wasteful or costly processes, improved customer service, better efficiency, and higher productivity. However, BPR should not be viewed as the mere automation of existing processes. Effective BPR will eliminate the wasteful elements of the process and then, if it appropriate, apply systems to deliver the automation and better overall efficiency.

Many of the most successful re-engineering projects have involved the introduction of electronic or paperless trading. Banks and building societies have introduced document image processing, where forms and letters are converted to digital images and processes using computers and work flow practices. There is no need to handle paper. Work loads can be balanced and managed so that maximum productivity and responsiveness to customer requirements is achieved.

In the retail and industrial sectors, examination of the processes involved in the manufacturing and supply chains have led to the application of electronic commerce concepts to streamline the supply chain. Concepts such as Electronic Data Interchange (EDI) have been applied to speed up communications between trading partners, effect the rapid payment of invoices, reduce other lead times and eliminate the cost and potential of errors associated with handling and processing huge amounts of paper.

Organisations considering embarking on re-engineering projects are well advised to talk to consultants and solutions providers with widespread experience in business analysis and re-engineering. These are most likely to have the breath of skills to make a holistic assessment of business processes and to deliver cost effective solutions based on the best available practices and technologies. As with so many parts of business life, careful planning and a clear set of objectives are also essential.

11. PROJECT PLANNING

There are many personal computer (PC) based tools and software which help with the management of a project and the allocation of responsibilities to software engineers.

It must be noted that the selection of a planning tool or package depends on what the IT department's study has highlighted; the usage and tasks the project control software package is supposed to cover.

The stages of development and the steps within each stage are recorded, together with the timescales and the staff involved. A Gantt chart is produced showing the dates applicable to the steps completed and those outstanding.

The updating is done regularly, preferably once a week and all participants become the recipients of various reports. Meetings are then held to discuss outstanding tasks, or issues arising.

To maintain an effective project control, the overall planning activity is supported by the project managers. The management forum sets priorities, allocates resources, resolves issues, and deals with risks.

The planning function relies on receiving up-to-date plans from individual project managers. As such, the planning office is responsible for the overall plan and the identification of risks and issues. Further on, the individual project plans, their monitoring, the transference of the actual resources and the reporting is handled by the planning office.

The plans are initiated by the Project Manager. These are then set up by the Planner. Once approved, the plans are maintained by the Planning/Project Office. The Planning Office personnel define the standards. Additionally, the planners are responsible for the development and maintenance of the integrated baseline plan.

Vital to the effective management of the programme are the plans with milestones, which:

- Set priorities,
- Allocate resources,
- Highlight issues,
- Assist in managing risks.

Timesheets are submitted on a weekly basis by the individuals in the project teams. Their completion is checked by the Project Manager. The details entered in the timesheets are transferred on the plans as actuals. The status of the plans is monitored by the Planning Office.

Regular reviews are held with the Project Managers. Following the reviews, the planner makes the necessary adjustments to the plans. When the adjustments are completed, copies with the appropriate changes are submitted to the Project Managers for approval.

The quality of the overall plan depends on the state of the plans of the individual teams and the commitment of the Project Managers to support this approach. With the outputs generated, the Project Manager identifies the resource requirements, the skills required to meet the targets and the costs incurred within the approved budget.

The Project Managers ensure that the:

- Plans are fit for the project,
- Current plans are logged,
- Plans and work completed match the project deadlines,
- Plans show adequate resources,
- Progress to date is in line with the expectations.

The project activities can include all the:

- IT applications,

- Embedded systems,
- Infrastructure,
- Equipment.

The Planning Office is responsible for the:

- Consistent standards on plans,
- Site plans development and maintenance,
- Agreement on milestones,
- Base lining of plans against actuals,
- Inter-projects dependencies.

The Planner works with individual Project Managers for the:

- Estimated and actual project costing,
- Planning training needs for the project teams,
- Monitoring of progress against milestones,
- Identification of contentions,
- Project issues and risks,
- Proposes solutions and corrective actions.

The planning tool deliverables include the:

- Plans with milestones (based on the individual team plans),
- A register of issues and risks and their impact on target dates.

The monitoring by the Planning Office enables the:

- Viewing,
- Tracking,
- Reporting.

  Viewing:

  - Production of Gantt charts,

- Fields to create new plans,
- Gantt by resource,
- Viewing of dependencies,
- Creation of new resources,
- Setting up and viewing of fixed loading patterns,
- Assigning of categories.

Tracking:

- Hours worked from time sheets,
- Actual end dates, Status and Complete,
- Timesheet per person,
- Timesheets for all resources,

Reporting:

- Gantt chart at task level,
- Gantt chart at phase level,
- Actuals against baseline effort,
- All project milestones,
- Total loading of resources in days per week,
- Tracked time by week,
- Estimate to complete,
- Subtotals by project within group.

In addition, the planner prepares all plans to show the following settings:

- Project,
- Phase activity,
- Task,
- Milestone.

Based on these settings the Planning Office outputs the following:

- Check list,
- Hierarchical chart,
- Programme flowchart,
- Weekly timesheets modifications,
- Individual project plans,
- Main plan.

The various stages of work within the projects are classified by site. Systems and tasks are allocated within the stages.

The tasks for the testing of the systems are uniform to all of the plans in the projects.

These are:

- Investigation,
- Risk Assessment,
- Review,
- Site Test Plan,
- Contingency Plan,
- Test,
- Documentation,
- Sign off.

The actuals recorded are based on the entry from the timesheets received from the Project Managers.

The start and end dates are locked and baselined. The base lining on the plans are:

- Non-production time,
- General project time,
- General project management tasks,

- Activities.

Where visits or tests on the sites have been completed, they are marked as milestones on the plans. Milestones are agreed with the Project Managers.

Based on the project managers' assumptions, estimates are entered on the plans. These estimates are initially baselined to show variances. The actuals are compared against these estimates.

All resources are allocated on the planned tasks. To enable quick tracking of loading, the resources are uniquely abbreviated.

The following sub-totals can be extracted from any of the project plans:

- **Resource loading,**
- **Elapsed time against phases,**
- **Sites,**
- **Systems.**

The following responsibilities are part of the planning service offered by the individual planners to the project in general:

- **Liaison with Project Managers,**
- **Co-ordination of all plans,**
- **Equal responsibility to all teams,**
- **Regular reviews with all Project Managers,**
- **Individual reviews,**
- **Global reviews (of all plans, at least every three months),**
- **Ad hoc presentations,**

Monitoring of:

- **Actuals,**
- **Appropriate dates,**

- Project milestones,
- All planning modifications,

Training on planning:

- Filtering,
- Production of plans,
- Timesheet entries,
- Conversions,

Collection of all estimates:

- Resource,
- Costs,
- Timescales.

The objective of using a planning tool, such as the Microsoft Project, PMW, or spreadsheets, is to produce plans and reports based on details submitted by the Project Managers. Some plans may already exist in a draft format, at detailed and summary level.

The completeness of the plans at the end of each period largely relies upon the input from the project teams. The Planner's responsibility is to verify the plans received and consequently standardise, rationalise and consolidate the plans entered by the individuals.

All project plans can be developed to a constant standard. Although there is a certain degree for local site control, the milestones can be agreed and all project plans can be baselined and monitored against actuals.

The planner demonstrates and advises on what already exists on the planning tool/s. Any changes to the planning practices rely on policy decisions made by senior management.

12. PROJECT MANAGEMENT WEAKNESSES

In the process of managing projects, it will soon become apparent that probably the main cause for threatening a project, are unidentified risks, or perhaps the weakness of individual/s to manage the growth of a system.

Even if you used I.T. Risk Management in its fullest, your experience will soon enable you to identify the real cause for the failure in implementing your system. In such cases, your programme/project management may need further support, assistance, training, better communicational ability and proper delegating, or even some listening to other people involved in the on-going project. Employing the expertise of a consultancy may help.

The main point is to try to reduce potential project caused loss by providing efficient *Event* driven project reviews for the critical project/s. Such project consulting steps will create and utilise virtual group of experienced project managers. As a panel of experts they will assess critical projects and provide consulting being perceived as helpful by the project team, the management, and the users/clients.

For such a project consulting programme implementation, various process steps are needed:

1. Select critical project,
2. Understand project status,
3. Plan project review,
4. Create reviews agenda
5. Execute project review,
6. Implement change plan,
7. Conclude the project review.

The project manager of the project pending the review should gather the requested information from the existing project documentation. If such documentation is not available, the project manager should collect as much as possible from verbal discussions.

Such a preparation should include details of:

1. Communication plans,
2. Project organisation plan,
3. Contacts and scopes,
4. Background and status of finances,

5. Schedules,

6. Status and history of resources plans,

7. Quality plan,

8. System documentation,

9. Brief description of the project environment,

10. Risk register prioritisation/s and other reports,

11. Last project review minutes.

The final outcome of all communications, discussions and reviews should enable the team members to produce an agreed score on the various project management resources.

The list for such a scoring agreement should include:

1. Quality management,

2. User participation,

3. Requirements management,

4. Communications,

5. Business orientation,

6. Project team,

7. Project planning,

8. Risk management,

9. Technical environment.

A scoring card graph can easily be produced on a spreadsheet and it ought to look something like the one shown on the next page:

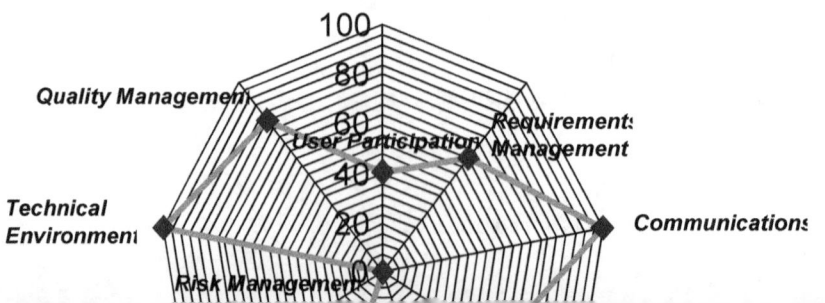

13. PROJECT MANAGEMENT POINTS

A risk is an uncertain event which may have an adverse effect on the project's objectives. Risk Management as a method is essential in managing and maintaining a successful project. It is essential that the project manager identifies the threatening risks throughout the project life-cycle.

The project manager must be:

- Forward looking, investigating problems and how to deal with threats,

- Must enable communication, getting people at all levels to talk to each other and to interact,

- Adopt a no blame team culture, bringing concerns into the open where actions can be taken and plans put in place, in order to stop a risk occurring.

The project management process commences by identifying the enterprises most important and risky projects, as these must be given priority.

This will include the varied events, their assessments, and the consequential risks relating to or consisting of a system. Methodical in procedures and plans, these are addressed to those involved and deliberating within the parameters of their systems development responsibilities.

The results will depend on interaction. The mutual or reciprocal action which encourages those involved in the programmes and projects to communicate with each other and to work closely with a view to solving the threatening events before they impact on the development of the system.

The individuals involved maintain a generic approach, which relates and characterises the whole group of those involved in assessing the events and attacking the threatening ones before they become risks to the development of the system; the end result being the avoidance of apparent problems within the pre-defined users' systems requirements.

This is enabled by following the highlighted principles of project management as described in the previous chapters of the '*MANAGE THAT I.T. PROJECT*' book.

The project managers, system architects, and the risk management practitioners simply follow the approved body of systems development methods, rules and management procedures employed by their organisation. For practical or even ethical reasons, it must be noted that with such a philosophy, it is seldom possible to fulfil all requirements of very large organisational systems.

As such, the project manager will need to adopt a proven systems methodology, which he/she can easily administer in applications. Putting to use such techniques and in applying the overall management principles in the development of various applications will involve numerous and varied activities.

A concrete issue in developing new applications is the problem of communication among the people involved, the motivation constantly needed for generic work, the ability to interact systematically and in using a structured systems methodology.

END

BIBLIOGRAPHY:

I.T. RISK MANAGEMENT, ISBN: 978-1-4467-5653-9
BUSINESS INFORMATION SYSTEMS, CONCEPTS AND EXAMPLES,
 ISBN: 978-1-4092-7338-7 & 0952795639
A GUIDE TO INFORMATION TECHNOLOGY,
 ISBN: 978-1-4092-7608-1 & 0952795647
CHANGE MANAGEMENT, ISBN: 978-1-4457-6114-5
CHANGE MANAGEMENT IN I.T.,
 ISBN: 978-1-4092-7712-5 & 0952725355
CHANGE MANAGEMENT IN SYSTEMS, ISBN: 978-1-4457-1099-0
FRONT-END DESIGN AND DEVELOPMENT FOR SYSTEMS APPLICATIONS
 ISBN: 978-1-4092-7588-6 & 0952725347
I.T RISK MANAGEMENT ISBN: 978-1-4092-7488-9 & 0952725320
THE SIMPLIFIED PROCEDURES FOR I.T. PROJECTS DEVELOPMENT,
 ISBN: 978-1-4092-7562-6 & 0952725312
THE SIGMA METHODOLOGY FOR RISK MANAGEMENT IN SYSTEMS
 DEVELOPMENT, ISBN: 978-1-4092-7690-6 & 095279568X
TRADING ON THE INTERNET IN THE YEAR 2000 AND BEYOND,
 ISBN: 978-1-4092- 7577 & 0952795671
STRUCTURED SYSTEMS METHODOLOGY ISBN: 978-1-4477-6610-0
SYSTEMS MANAGEMENT, ISBN: 978-1-4710-4907-1,
 978-1-4710-4891-3, 978-1-4710-4903-3
INFORMATION TECHNOLOGY LOGICAL ANALYSIS,
 ISBN: 978-1-4717-1688-1
I.T. RISKS LOGICAL ANALYSIS, ISBN: 978-1-4717-1957-8
I.T. CHANGES LOGICAL ANALYSIS, ISBN: 978-1-4717-2288-2
LOGICAL ANALYSIS OF SYSTEMS, RISKS, CHANGES,
 ISBN: 978-1-4717-2294-3
MANAGEMENT OF I.T. CHANGES, RISKS, WORKSHOPS,
 EPISTEMOLOGY, ISBN: 978-1-84753-147-6
THE MANAGEMENT OF COMMERCIAL COMPUTING,
 ISBN: 978-1-4092-7550-3 & 0952795604
PROGRAMME MANAGEMENT WORKSHOP,
 ISBN: 978-1-4092-7583-1& 0952725371
THE PHILOSOPHICAL CONCEPTS OF MANAGEMENT THROUGH THE
 AGES, ISBN: 978-1-4092- 7554-1 & 0952725363
THE MANAGEMENT OF PROJECTS, SYSTEMS, INTERNET, AND RISKS,
 ISBN: 978-1-4092- 7464-3 & 0952795698
HOW TO CONSTRUCT YOUR RESUMÊ, ISBN: 978-1-4092-7383-7
SYSTEMS ENGINEERING, ISBN: 978-1-4477-7553-9

www.ingramcontent.com/pod-product-compliance
Lightning Source LLC
Chambersburg PA
CBHW071615170526
45166CB00003B/1086